Richard and Anna Newcomb House

HISTORIC QUINCY ARCHITECTURE

ARCHITECTURAL TREASURES OF QUINCY, ILLINOIS

PHOTOGRAPHY BY RICHARD PAYNE
TEXT BY PAUL CLIFFORD LARSON
FOREWORD BY CARL LANDRUM
INTRODUCTION BY JAMES B. STEWART

PRODUCED BY GEORGE M. IRWIN
EDITED BY CLARISSE BURNS
DESIGNED BY JERRY HERRING

PUBLISHED BY HERRING PRESS
1996

Published by
Herring Press
1216 Hawthorne
Houston, Texas 77006
(713) 526-1250

Editing by Clarisse Burns
Design by Jerry Herring
Production Coordination by
  Laura Dignazio
Color Separations by Emmott-Walker
  Printing, Inc., Houston, Texas
Printing in Canada by Friesens

ISBN Number 0-917001-11-7

Library of Congress
Catalog Card Number:
96-76737

For additional books, send $35
plus $4 for shipping and handling to:

Quincy Society of Fine Arts
Oakley-Lindsay Center
300 Civic Center Plaza
Suite 244
Quincy, Illinois 62301

Park Place

For years Quincyans have benefitted from living, working, studying, and worshipping in buildings that, in themselves, contribute to the quality of life we call the American Dream. Quincy's architecture from the 1830's through the 1930's is impressive. Over the years, master builders, contractors, and out-of-town and local architects have contributed to the inventory. The high percentage of home ownership and locally owned businesses has enhanced our streetscapes. Even though growth patterns, fires, and tornados have destroyed some magnificent nineteenth-century landmarks, the quality and quantity of the remaining architecture make it a source of pride for its users.

A chance visit to Quincy, Illinois, in May 1993 by architectural photographer Richard Payne and editor Clarisse Burns was the stimulus that turned a dream into reality with the publication of this book of color photographs of Quincy's historic architecture. In the development of this project, we felt that something more than the publication of a long-needed book should be part of the goal. A steering committee was formed, drawing its representatives from nine local cultural groups in the fields of architecture and other visual arts, which contributed to the prepublication fund that assured the book's publication. Other civic leaders also served on the committee; more than 100 contributors generously responded.

Architectural historian Paul Clifford Larson was chosen to write the principal essay and to undertake the research on each of the buildings. Quincy's Pulitzer Prize-winning author James B. Stewart has recorded his observations, and longtime Quincy historian Carl Landrum reflects on men and events in Quincy's colorful past. In a second collaboration, photographer Richard Payne worked with publisher Herring Press, both of Houston, Texas, to record this selection from Quincy's remarkable architectural tradition. In telling our story of Quincy, we also include photographs of some "lost Quincy" landmarks, chosen from the libraries of the Gardner Museum of Architecture & Design and the Historical Society of Quincy and Adams County.

The publication of this book was made possible by a major grant from the Quincy Foundation. Special contributors include Architechnics, Inc.; Mr. and Mrs. Lawrence J. Cervon; Mrs. Patricia Gardner Cleek; Coldwell Banker/Mays Real Estate, Inc.; Coleman Motor Company, Inc.; Dr. and Mrs. Merle F. Crossland; Louis DeGreeff and Marilyn Burns; Gardner Denver Machinery Inc.; Guardtree Limited/Quincy Development Center; Hansen-Spear Funeral Directors, Ltd.; William and Susan P. Holliday; George M. Irwin; Marion Gardner Jackson Charitable Trust; Marion Gardner Jackson Arts Fund/Quincy Society of Fine Arts; KHQA TV, The Knapheide Manufacturing Co.; Mrs. A.O. Lindsay, Jr.; Little River Development Co.; Richard and Patti McNay; Quincy Metal Fabricators, Inc.; The Quincy Herald-Whig; John and Carolyn Stevenson; Stillwell Foundation; Mrs. Maurice M. Taylor; Mrs. Henry B. Weis; WGEM AM-FM-TV; In Memory of Barbara Lindsay Williams; and Dennis R. Williams.

The nine participating organizations that will share in the proceeds from sales of this book are Friends of the Dr. Richard Eells House, Gardner Museum of Architecture & Design, German Village Society, Historical Society of Quincy and Adams County, Quincy Art Center, Quincy Preservation Commission/City of Quincy, Quincy Preserves, Quincy Society of Fine Arts, and The Quincy Museum. They are also special contributors.

Certainly, the publication of *Historic Quincy Architecture* has been a cooperative community project.

PROJECT STEERING
COMMITTEE

George M. Irwin
Chairman

Mariann Barnard
Joe Bonansinga
Nancy Brinkman
Reaugh Broemmel
Marilyn Burns
Joe Conover
Marcia Cray
Rob Dwyer
Philip Germann
Doris Hoener
Carol Mason
Robert A. Mays
Peter A. Oakley
Mary Catherine Paben
Pattie Paxton
Ridgely Pierson
Sharon Zimmerman

Park Place

1400 Block of Maine Street

400 Block of Hampshire Street

Woodland Cemetery

As a city of stately old homes and fine business buildings, grassy lawns and bountiful trees, Quincy reflects the tastes and habits of the early settlers who populated it, many from the New England states. Early immigrants came looking for a new home and a chance to continue the trades they had learned in the Old World. Some came up from New Orleans, perhaps stopping for a while in St. Louis before locating permanently in Quincy. Others came by way of the Ohio River, then up the Mississippi River, from Virginia and Kentucky.

Many of the early large homes of Quincy were built on the bluffs overlooking the Mississippi River and adjacent to the commercial area surrounding the square. By the 1850's, as the city grew and prospered, the population moved east. John Wood's magnificent stone octagon mansion and I. O. Woodruff's imposing brick residence are now remembered only in photographs. But many other homes remain: those of Lorenzo Bull, Charles Henry Bull, William S. Warfield, Richard F. Newcomb, Theodore C. Poling, David W. Miller, and James T. Baker, all nineteenth-century landmarks.

Political persons who came to Quincy from Virginia and Kentucky were Orville H. Browning and James W. Singleton. Browning had an elaborate home at Seventh and Hampshire, where many famous people, including his friend Abraham Lincoln, were entertained. Singleton owned an Italian Villa Style residence known as Boscobel, northeast of Quincy, which at one time was described as the most expensive and elegant private residence in this section of the state. Probably the most outstanding political figure in Quincy's early days was Stephen A. Douglas, who held court in Quincy and maintained a law office in the Quincy House. Douglas never owned a private residence, but he is noted for his participation in the trial of Dr. Richard Eells, accused of helping an escaped slave in 1842, and, of course, for the senatorial debates with Lincoln in 1858.

Starting in 1829, many of Quincy's buildings were constructed of brick made in Quincy brickyards. Some of Quincy's smaller, older brick homes on the south side of the city, an area usually known as Calftown, were built by citizens who came here from Germany to escape military conscription.

Along with the numerous great homes built over the years, there were other imposing structures as well: the Quincy House, the Opera House, the Adams County Courthouse, the Quincy City Hall, the Chicago, Burlington and Quincy Depot, the Presbyterian Church, the Congregational Church, St. Peter's Church, and St. Boniface Church, all now gone because of storm, fire, or demolition. Existing landmarks from this period include the Salem Evangelical Church, St. John the Baptist Catholic Church, the Ricker National Bank, and Temple B'nai Sholom.

Outstanding Quincy builders were Buerkin and Kaempen, who built the high school, now in use as the junior high school, at 14th and Maine. Other builders were William Larkworthy, Eaton Littlefield, and a Mr. Bangs, who helped move John Wood's Greek Revival mansion across 12th Street in 1864—without damaging a tall hedge!

For years, the tobacco industry furnished employment for many Quincy men, and only the purchase of these companies by the large cigarette firms brought that industry to a close. The last to leave was the Wellman and Dwire Tobacco Company. Robert Gardner came to Quincy to work in a machine shop at Sixth and Maine and went on to found the large manufacturing company known as Gardner–Denver Company, still in existence.

The Fisher brothers started a stove repair business at Third and Delaware, which grew into a major stove manufacturing concern housed in a large building at Front and Ohio. At the end of the nineteenth century, Quincy was the leading stove manufacturing center in the nation.

The three Dick brothers came to America from Germany, stopping off in Alton, Illinois, before continuing to a home in Iowa. They stayed in Quincy long enough to discover the cold, bubbling springs at Ninth and York, where in 1856 they bought the site and erected their first brewery. Soon their product was being shipped all over the region. Theirs was one of six breweries that flourished in Quincy over the years.

Transportation into Quincy, both by river and by rail, had much to do with the city's progress. During earlier days, when pork packing was a big industry, pork was shipped by rail from Quincy to Chicago and New York. River packets carried passengers and freight from St. Louis, Missouri, to St. Paul, Minnesota, stopping off in Quincy.

It is a tribute to those responsible for the construction of the early homes and business and public buildings in Quincy—the architects, contractors, and laboring men—that these buildings have withstood the ravages of time. Many who visit Quincy these days and see the fine old homes are especially impressed with the architecture. With the loving care of their current and future owners, they no doubt will continue to stand for many years.

Historic Quincy Architecture gives us an excellent look at Quincy's diverse architecture and its architectural achievements from the 1830's through the 1930's.

Carl Landrum

1600 Block of York Street

I'm not sure just how old I was when I realized Quincy wasn't like other Midwestern cities. Maybe it was a trip to Battle Creek, Michigan, a typical factory town, bleak and uninspiring. Perhaps it was a visit to Southampton, New York, where tourists gape at mansions that are no grander than those I grew up with. Having spent nearly all of the first 18 years of my life in Quincy, I took its architecture, its setting above the river, its shady streets, for granted.

I walked to Adams School, with its huge windows, along 20th Street, lined with trees and modest, tidy houses. I loved the old public library at Fourth and Maine, with its turreted staircase leading to the children's department and its musty smell of books. Driving by 18th and Maine, I'd fantasize about living inside the sprawling stone house on the southwest corner. I loved the rumble of car wheels on brick-paved Jersey Street and Park Place. I didn't yet realize it, but Quincy is a place that feeds the imagination.

Having lived elsewhere, I now savor Quincy on every visit. Surely everyone appreciates the downtown square, the wide expanse of Maine Street lined with mansions, the East End Historic District, the John Wood mansion. Yet, on each visit, I see other parts of Quincy in a new and appreciative light: streets like South 22nd Street, its spacious width lined with well-kept homes that speak so eloquently of the American dream; North Fifth Street, with its old brick houses and faded elegance; Ridgewood and Edgewood drives, with their sleek, low houses that must reflect the vision of a Fifties modernist. I hope this tradition continues.

I have seen Quincy change over the years, as it must. The small neighborhood grocery stores and bakeries have vanished. Downtown is a shadow of what it was when I was a child. Will malls, superstores, and four-lane highways ever be designated for historic preservation? And why must new houses be so large, with such prominent garages? Such "progress" has always been a visitor to Quincy, yet the character of the town survives.

How fortunate for Quincy that it has so many people who obviously care about their homes, their gardens, their schools, and the fabric of the community. So many older homes and buildings seem to have been rescued and invested with new life. I read in the national press about planned residential towns, like Seaside and Celebration in Florida, that are using architecture to try to recapture a sense of community, while Quincy seems never to have lost its own. I realize now that Quincy is unusual and fortunate to have such vivid architectural reminders of its past without being a museum or Colonial reproduction. It gives everyone who lives or has lived in Quincy a better sense of themselves.

I am sure that *Historic Quincy Architecture* will deepen the awareness of Quincy's rich architectural heritage, not just locally, but throughout the country. Quincy deserves to be known and appreciated.

James B. Stewart

THE ARCHITECTURAL HERITAGE OF QUINCY, ILLINOIS

AN HISTORICAL OVERVIEW

BY PAUL CLIFFORD LARSON

The city of Quincy, Illinois, is a national treasure. Situated on an Illinois bluff overlooking the Mississippi River, its architecture captures 100 years of American building practice at its best. History has left a trail everywhere: in the brick immigrant cottages of the south side, the grand turn-of-the-century houses of the east end, the rich mix of periods and styles of the north side, and the monumental stone facades embracing its central square.

Quincy traces its beginnings to 1821, when an adventurer from New York by the name of John Wood spotted the high bluffs and natural harbor and wrote to a friend that he wanted "to settle here for life." An elevation above the periodic flooding and "pestilence" of the river bottoms and easy dockage for steamboats were a rare combination; this was the first site north of St. Louis, Missouri, to boast them. In December of the following year, Wood made good on his declaration by building a log cabin at the base of the bluffs. Four years after his first visit, he and his frequent companion, Willard Keyes, together with a small band of settlers, formally established the village of Quincy, with John's Square as its central park and Adams as its county, all after names of the recently elected President.

The area laid out for the new village comprised 235 lots on rolling terrain, many with spectacular views of the river. But these aesthetic virtues were detriments to rapid settlement, for a perch over 100 feet above the river and a network of ravines posed problems for transport to and within the settlement. As a young settler wrote to his father, "Climbing the bluff twice a day together with other business gives one plenty of exercise." Wood's and Keyes's own houses were crude log cabins located at the foot of

Adams County Courthouse
JOHN MCKEAN, ARCHITECT

1876-1949

the bluff, just above the normal spring flood line, and on two of the few existing approaches to the heights above.

Incorporation as a town in 1834 produced the public financing necessary to overcome the community's geographical hazards and inconveniences. The 1825 village of 16 inhabitants quickly became a town of 500; by 1840 it had grown into a city of 2,300. The population tripled again by 1850, then doubled in each of the following decades. By 1870, Quincy was the second-leading city in Illinois.

The greatest initial spur to growth was the location in Quincy of a U.S. Land Office in 1835. The young town was the best port in the vast west-central stretch of Illinois set apart as bounty land for veterans of the War of 1812. Few veterans settled in the Quincy area, but their agents flocked to the land office, many of them doubling as dealers in private land. Small-town New England provided the first wave of settlement, while a handful of German immigrants in the late 1830's grew to 10,000 by the end of the 1860's. These settlers were joined by intermittent bands of Kentuckians, Irish immigrants who came to work on the railroads, and a sudden influx of African-Americans from Missouri and points south in the aftermath of the Civil War. The manufacture of such local necessities as stoves, wagons, packing boxes, and agricultural supplies and implements soon mushroomed into industries of national scope and prominence, while Quincy also became a major regional supplier of such commodities as pork and ice. By mid-century, Quincy had also emerged as an important center of political activity, with such national figures as Stephen A. Douglas, O. H. Browning, and W. A. Richardson practicing law there in the early years of their careers.

For all its rapid early growth and thriving economy, Quincy was never a boom town in the usual sense. It boasted no great natural resource, such as lumber or mineral deposits, and was not on a major supply route for westward expansion. Easterners and German immigrants flocked to Quincy, not because of visions of quick profit, great natural resources, or even a thriving labor market, but simply because they wanted to live there and saw prospects for long-term success. The great high-style building campaigns of the late 1860's, 1880's, and World War I era were practically devoid of speculation. Each was supported by generations of economic stability and prosperity.

By the late 1880's, the beauty and prosperity of the city had captured widespread eastern attention, though there was some disagreement as to whether the extraordinary stability of the city's wealth was an asset or a mark of stagnation. Two feature pictorials in the popular Frank Leslie's "Illustrated Weekly," both issued in 1890, took opposite points of view. One lampooned the city for a bonded indebtedness equal to one-third of the city's assessed value, the high taxes that went along with it, and a stranglehold that a few "Shylocks" had put on the railroad business. The other commended the city for its "steady substantial growth for over sixty years," resulting in "more the substantial, well-built air of an eastern city than is often found in the west."

When overland transport replaced the river as the great connective tissue between cities, Quincy's halcyon days were destined to come to an end. For a while, it looked as if the city might overcome its late start in railroading. A new Chicago, Burlington and Quincy Railroad Depot arose in 1899, sized to serve a city of 200,000 people. Four years later an equally magnificent depot was built for the Wabash Line. But visions of regional dominance, of a Chicago on the Mississippi, never came to fruition. New rail linkage offered at best little more than an interesting detour in the quadrangle formed by Chicago,

Wabash Railway Depot
THEODORE LINK, ARCHITECT

1903-1964

St. Louis, Kansas City, and St. Paul. The great routes west had already developed, and Quincy was not on them. The 1939 WPA Guide to Illinois expressed Quincy's plight with a single statistic: "Industrial and agricultural products that had formerly found an outlet in the holds of 40 steamers shrank to the capacity of a single spur line of the railroad." Wagons, stoves, and wooden incubators lost their national market and, like immigrant culture, were absorbed into the workaday world of another medium-sized Midwestern city.

Quincy's long period of economic stability, its freedom from the boom-or-bust conditions that wrought such sudden changes in the human geography of the Midwest, accounts more than any other factor for the preservation of so many layers of its building stock. Personal prosperity took years to arrive, and when it came, new neighborhoods were created, leaving the old intact. Only in the expanding downtown were buildings regularly upgraded or replaced, and this process came to a halt before the Great Depression of this century. Conversely, when steamboat transport fell off, or the railroads left, prosperity remained, along with the buildings that were its most visible expression. The result was an architectural legacy built up in increments, giving permanent and equal voice to the aspirations, tastes, and living requirements of five generations.

No architectural legacy can be sustained without the support of a proud and vigilant citizenry. Between 1835 and 1950, Quincyans watched over the buildings of their city as if they were part of themselves, replacing only those lost to catastrophe, severe deterioration, or expansion of the commercial center. In the aftermath of World War I, a generalized contempt for simple cottages, paired with a distaste for High Victorian embellishment, resulted in the fragmentation of many of America's most distinctive nineteenth-century neighborhoods, but not in Quincy. Homeowners with a yearning for modernization settled for a porch replacement, leaving the house behind it unaltered. Even post-

World War II modernism, with its aggressive vision of cities rebuilt to the latest specifications, arrived tardily and ineffectually. Plans for a downtown make over failed to get the economic and political support for more than a scattering of new construction and face-lifts.

The greatest danger to Quincy's legacy has come in the last two decades as the population and economic base of the city have shifted to the suburbs. But even when the downtown and the once-fashionable north side entered a period of decline, a new preservation consciousness dawned in the east end, and the south side rediscovered its German heritage. Most of the historic downtown and south side, and much of the east end, are now National Register districts, comprising over 3,000 buildings in all; a north-side district is also in the offing. With a brightening of economic conditions, the downtown is on the upswing again. Several north-side neighborhoods are showing signs of the social vitality and autonomous spirit that created so rich an architectural mix in the last century and that continue to make the district the most varied in the city.

John Wood's Octagon House
JOHN M. VAN OSDEL, ARCHITECT

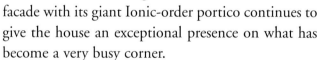

1860-1950

THE RUDIMENTS OF A CITY

Early settlers could hardly have anticipated the architectural splendors the village would one day achieve. Makeshift log cabins, plank-sided, timber-framed cottages, and quickly thrown-up commercial fronts were the staple of the first thousand arrivals, from John Wood's cabin of 1822 straight through the 1840's. Aesthetic relief, and an inkling of the future, was principally afforded by a scattering of small "permanent" houses and stores made of local brick.

Against this backdrop, typical of a nascent Midwestern town, Quincy erected three soaring monuments in the mid-1830's, when the nation as a whole was in the economic doldrums. A colonnaded and towered county courthouse reigned over John's Square, while the Quincy House, a palatial hotel built with eastern money and local skepticism, anchored the southwest corner. The third exceptional building was John Wood's first mansion at what was then the eastern edge of town. All were a variant of the Greek Revival Style.

The buildings on the square burned to the ground in 1875 and 1883, but the John Wood mansion remains. Designed and constructed by master builder John Cleaveland between 1835 and 1838, it has been painstakingly restored by its owner of nearly 100 years, the Historical Society of Quincy and Adams County. Originally fronting State Street on the block to the west, by the 1860's the house had come to mark the termination of the German immigrant commercial corridor running from the river to 11th Street. It was moved to its present site after Wood decided to build an even larger mansion, an octagon of stone, just behind it. The Octagon House has disappeared, but Cleaveland's masterful handling of the earlier mansion's facade with its giant Ionic-order portico continues to give the house an exceptional presence on what has become a very busy corner.

That the John Wood mansion should have survived is hardly surprising, for it has long been revered as the home of the central figure of Quincy's early history. Lloyd and Mercy Morton's house on Broadway is another matter altogether: Morton was one of a small group of eastern land developers who leap-frogged their way across Illinois to Adams County. He erected, east of the town limits, cottages reminiscent of eighteenth-century New England but enlivened with Greek Revival details. The other cottages have long since disappeared, but Morton's suburban cottage still stands as a lonely sentinel of the distant past in the midst of a 1920's residential neighborhood that is itself threatened by commercial development. Built in 1837, Morton's naively designed cottage is also a wonderful complement to the grandeur of the house of his more famous contemporary.

One of Quincy's great natural advantages, shared

by many Mississippi River settlements, was extensive deposits of shale clay and, immediately beneath, a bed of hard limestone. By the late 1840's, local brick manufacture from the clay was widespread, much of it occurring in makeshift open kilns located within several feet of the house being built. At the same time, extensive limestone quarries opened south of Quincy. Brick houses on stone foundations began to typify the fledgling city, and the downtown square grew its first high-grade commercial row, a cluster of unadorned three-story brick buildings adapted from common residential types.

Vernacular construction continued to be the rule well into the 1850's, with scarcely a hint of the high style expressed by the John Wood mansion and the Quincy House. Plain red brick surfaces with regularly spaced window and door openings, each headed with a brick arch or a simple stone lintel, were the hallmarks of local house building. Occasional hints of the Greek Revival enlivened the larger or more expensive homes with such details as a half-round attic window, prominent gable returns (fancifully known as broken pediment), or a narrow strip of windows surrounding the entry. This melding of simple vernacular forms with fragments of neoclassicism hinted at the Federal Style popular in New England at the beginning of the century, but the vernacular buildings lacked even the smallest touches of door, window, and cornice ornamentation that graced the formative examples of that style.

View of streetscape east of Washington Park
c. 1858

Vernacular buildings tend to be differentiated principally by their plan, with four types paramount in Quincy prior to the Civil War. The most common one-story, or cottage, type was the hall-and-parlor, consisting of two side-by-side rooms facing the street; the most common two-story type had a side hall and stairway and one room on each floor. Since the size of the house depended on the number of rooms, not the number of stories, a second story simply indicated a preference for greater privacy between the rooms. If more size were desired, either type could be modified into a double-stack plan by stretching the house or cottage to the rear. From the outset, New Englander, Irish, and German builders constructed their houses the same; they used the same plans and built with the same methods and materials.

THE TRIUMPH OF STYLE

Stylistically sophisticated architecture finally began to be seen in Quincy during the early 1850's, as Eastern speculation in Midwestern land and buildings (among other things) ballooned. Coincidentally, this period was also marked by the peak of German immigration into Quincy and, perhaps more to the point, by the accumulation of a sufficient level of wealth by New England-born merchants and capitalists to let them show it off a bit. The Italianate Style, which had been popular for nearly a decade on the seaboard, was the first to display its charms in town. For the Bull brothers, who had come to Quincy as teenagers nearly 20 years before, the Italianate Style was the perfect vehicle for capturing the ethos of country squires on their new land in the east end. In 1856, Lorenzo Bull's captain's walk and Charles Bull's belvedere were still novelties in a town that was soon to sprout as many such rooftop adornments as it then had steeples and smokestacks.

A growing circle of master builders, headed by pioneer carpenters George Baumann and Eaton Littlefield, and more recent arrivals Frederick Reinecker and William Hauworth, soon began to fill the better neighborhoods with bracketed, cupolaed, high-windowed specimens of the new Italianate Style. Even vernacular buildings began to show its influence: round-headed windows popped up in street facades, and keystones were inserted into common segmental arches. Porches with elaborate millwork became commonplace, either as new construction or as a cheap remodeling. The simplest box on a 30-foot lot was allowed to acquire the romantic look of a Downing suburban villa. Social pressures must also have come into play, as several of the city's elite citizens transformed their vernacular, mildly Greek Revival houses into full-blown specimens of the Italianate manner, complete with bracketed cornices, tall and elaborately hooded windows, and expansive verandas.

The financial crash of 1855 ruined a number of local fortunes, but it did little to quell the general confidence that Quincy was a city of destiny. John's Square was renamed Washington Park in time for the Lincoln-Douglas Debate of 1858, and several of the buildings fronting it had face-lifts. By the outbreak of the Civil War, the city's already vaunted natural beauty was being complemented by a growing strain of architectural elegance. New residential corridors to the north and east were dominated by mansions with an air of artistry. When the war put a hold on the better class of residential construction, the downtown continued to build up, with the grandest commercial construction reserved for the immediate aftermath of the war. By the time of the next depression in 1873, cornices with scrolled brackets lined Washington Park and Maine Street to the east and had begun to pop up on the corner markets and saloons of the north and south sides.

The Italianate Style exerted so strong a hold on local builders that few ventures were made in competing styles until well after the Civil War. Farther east, and in many other Midwestern towns, Gothic cottages swept in with Italianate mansions; the two were often publicized in the same pattern books. But in Quincy, nearly 20 years separated the influx of the Italianate and the Gothic. The single exception was St. John's Episcopal Church, an English Gothic building closely akin to the work of famed New York architect Richard Upjohn. The parish had, in fact, hired Upjohn to design their church in 1851 but were aghast at both his fees and the cost of the projected building; the following year they turned to a local architect.

A breakthrough into the growing trove of national

First Presbyterian Church
ROBERT BUNCE, ARCHITECT

1879-1976

styles, and the eclecticism that mixed them, required outside intervention, which came after the Civil War when a nationwide burst of building activity brought eastern architects into Midwestern towns previously untouched by their profession. Robert Bunce arrived in Quincy in 1867 or 1868 after a short tenure in Chicago, followed by John S. McKean in 1874. Bunce was directly or indirectly responsible for scores of elaborate Italianate commercial blocks in the city; a half-dozen of the earliest got his name attached to them in print, while many of the rest could as easily be the result of copying by Reinecker or the other skilled local master builders. Bunce also introduced the full-blown Second Empire Style in an 1872 residence, though it had been fashionable to cap Italianate houses with French roofs since the Civil War. Bunce's versatility was most conspicuous in his church designs of the early 1870's. Rather than settling on a single mode of design, he adapted style to congregation: high-steepled Gothic for German Evangelicals, an approximation of English-parish Gothic for New England Congregationalists, shingled Gothic for High Church Episcopalians (who saved their money for the interior), a raised-basement Romanesque for African Methodists, and Islamic Revival for the Hebrew Congregation.

Bunce was the true father of Quincy's architecture, not simply by dint of training and personal accomplishments: he also began two lines of succession that would enrich the city's streetscapes and neighborhoods through the 1930's. One of his apprentices, Quincy native Harvey Chatten, was a talented designer who brought the Queen Anne Style to its greatest local realization. Chatten, in turn, trained Ernest Wood, the leading practitioner of the Prairie Style. Another Bunce apprentice was Frank Tubbesing, also a Quincy native. Tubbesing was of a lesser talent but extraordinarily prolific; his simple buildings form a sound, unpretentious backdrop for the more elaborate commissions of his contemporaries. Tubbesing's apprentice, Martin J. Geise, performed much the same function for the next generation.

Robert Bunce's only real competition in the 1870's was John S. McKean. Though McKean's tenure in Quincy was short, spanning only the years from 1874 to 1878, he left behind four of the city's finest High Victorian monuments. His single greatest achievement was the new Adams County Courthouse. Built in 1876, it came to lord it over a magnificently landscaped square at the northern edge of downtown, until a tornado in 1945 took off its dome and the county decided to build anew. The year 1876 also gave rise to the city's two most accomplished Second Empire designs, a bank for local financial magnate H. J. F. Ricker and a house for sewing machine salesman Dricus Snitjer. McKean's role in the former is certain; in the latter, attributed. McKean's final great gift to the city was Salem Evangelical Church, a finely detailed Victorian Gothic design erected at the heart of the wealthiest sector of the German immigrant community. All of these buildings rose from the trough of the nation's worst economic depression since 1855, and all but the courthouse have survived to undergo sympathetic restorations in recent years.

Franklin School
ROBERT BUNCE, ARCHITECT

1870-1905

In 1883, as critical an observer as Mark Twain called Quincy a "model New England town" with "broad, clean streets, trim, neat dwellings and lawns, fine mansions, [and] stately blocks of commercial buildings." By the time Twain made his observations, Bunce and McKean had both departed for larger cities, leaving local building design largely in the hands of Quincy's native sons. But the flow of lavish new architecture continued unabated.

Sixth Street to the north, and Maine and Hampshire streets to the east, all began to fill with hybrids of the Italianate, Gothic, Second Empire, and Queen Anne styles. Most were built in the "substantial" and "handsome" manner noted by Twain, with only isolated excursions into the bric-a-brac

componentry that would eventually anathematize the Queen Anne Style to serious architects and the American public at large. In fact, Quincy's few examples of High Victorian architecture at its most eclectic and dysfunctional can generally be traced to pattern-book designs such as those of New Yorker George Palliser and Chicagoan George Garnsey. The eccentric chimney placement and swollen Moorish tower of Chatten's design for the Isaac Lesem house, for example, bear a striking resemblance to a published Garnsey plan; other Garnsey and Palliser plans with half-pediments on shed roofs, elaborate, gabled dormers at the peaks of attics, and chimneys pierced by windows were more completely realized, each providing a sort of heady relief to the more abstemious work typical of Quincy architects.

Increasing financial and commercial ties to Chicago inevitably brought with them more commissions by that city's architects. J. Lyman Silsbee, a distinguished architect remembered today chiefly (and unfairly) as Frank Lloyd Wright's first employer, was hired by local grocery wholesaler William S. Warfield to build a superbly detailed mansion in the reigning style for those with money to spend, the Richardsonian Romanesque. With this foothold in the east end, Silsbee moved across the side street to design a carriage house and a new library for Lorenzo Bull and an expansive Shingle Style house for Bull's son, William. While Silsbee was under contract, Bull also hired a Chicago competitor, Patton and Fisher, to design a public library for the city; three years later he and his brother hired the same firm to design a new building for their State Savings Loan and Trust Co. Both were located on Washington Park, and both were in the Richardsonian Romanesque Style. The final Chicago-based design may have been the finest of all, D. H. Burnham and Company's ill-fated Chicago, Burlington & Quincy Railroad Depot erected in 1899. Probably designed several years earlier, it was on a par with Burnham and Root's best work of the early 1890's.

By 1889, local architects Harvey Chatten and John Batschy had learned enough elements of Richardson's style to slip Romanesque foundations under their Queen Anne houses; two years later they began producing entire buildings in the style. Chatten's design for Richard F. Newcomb, who lived across the street from William S. Warfield, is a virtual encyclopedia of Richardson's sources and one of the most elaborate, if not the most unified, examples of his style in the state. Batschy's masterpiece was the city's one towering loss to the modernist impulses of the 1960's: a massive commercial block housing Gem City Business College and embellished with wide belts and friezes of hand-tooled terra cotta.

Through all of the great building years of the 1880's and early 1890's, Quincy's newspapers denied that the city had anything so ephemeral as a boom going on; what was happening here was more substantial, more lasting, and—here was the important point—just a step on the city's sure march to major significance. For all the city's railroading woes, many still believed a population of 100,000 was not far away. Spurred by this sense of optimism, developers imitated the exclusive residential schemes of the larger cities. In 1889, an old outlot was carved into a covenanted neighborhood less than a mile from downtown. Dubbing it Park Place, its developers required occupants to build two-story houses of brick or stone, spend at least $5,000, and place their houses on a standardized setback. Lawndale, a more eastern development of 1890, lacked these restrictions, but its curving roads and large lots attracted magnificent architect-designed homes for two generations.

THE BEGINNINGS OF MODERNISM

The nearly universal American repentance for the excesses of late nineteenth-century taste crept into Quincy slowly, never arriving in some quarters at all; through the 1930's, Chamber of Commerce publications showed the pretentious mansions of the past along-

Gem City Business College
JOHN BATSCHY, ARCHITECT

1892-1968

side the bungalows and boxes currently in style. The major impetus for change may, in fact, have come from within the local architectural profession itself rather than from public pressure. In George Behrensmeyer, the city produced its first academically trained architect; he returned from the University of Illinois in 1892 fully armed with the Colonial Revival and a retooled version of the Queen Anne styles. Ernest Wood, though he never had architectural training outside of Chatten's office, must have re-educated himself after striking out on his own; by 1906 he started to introduce the mannerisms of suburban Chicago architects George Maher and Frank Lloyd Wright into his houses. Martin J. Geise, in the meantime, produced some of the city's first bungalows while picking up clues from his local competitors for larger house designs.

Since Quincy's first native architects began practice only in the late 1870's, they were forced with their former apprentices to make the difficult transition into the modern periods. Their success was erratic at best, for none was able completely to shed the sensibility of Victorian architectural models. Batschy leapt into the new gospel of rectilinearity but floundered when attempting to dress up the boxes. Chatten created in the new manner by stripping ornament off the old, never quite catching hold of the Craftsman idea of structure itself as ornament. His most successful twentieth-century buildings are curious transplants of Victorian styles into Craftsman ground, such as the sprawling Shingle Style-influenced P. H. Gardner house and the picturesque Queen Anne-influenced Unitarian Church. His fellow Bunce apprentice, Frank Tubbesing, could not grasp where to go apart from the simplifications he had already made to the Queen Anne Style and died prematurely, chagrined that he had not made more of a mark in his profession.

Stylistic purity was no more a requisite for success with the new breed of architects than it had been for their predecessors. The most characteristic designs of the period were Craftsman in tenor but filled with

Prairie Style touches. Behrensmeyer liked to mix in English detailing of the Arts and Crafts Movement, such as heavily molded entry porticos and geometrical stone inlays. Wood proved capable of Prairie Style designs of the purest order in a number of houses for out-of-town clients, but in Quincy itself, only his own office and studio building stuck to the Wrightian model. Wood's designs for Quincy clients clustered windows into bands and thrust out horizontal wings in Wright's fashion, but they eschewed casement windows and stuck to ornamental devices popular within the Craftsman movement as a whole. Both architects also worked in the neoclassical vein required for commercial projects or for clients who were clamoring for Colonial Revival. But the Craftsman spirit was always present, if not in the treatment of ornament, then in the choice of local stone or unmatched brick for facings, or of Mission Style interior casework.

Chicago, Burlington & Quincy Depot
D. H. BURNHAM AND COMPANY, ARCHITECTS

1899-1962

The story of American architecture has one chapter missing in Quincy: the Roaring Twenties never brought the great flowering of period styles that spread through the country-club suburbs of the rest of the nation's cities. A handful of Tudor Revival houses, and one or two in a Mediterranean vein, sprang up in the east end, but these lack the storybook quality that was *de rigueur* for builders who rejected Colonial Revival during the years preceding the Great Depression. Walter Stevenson's romantic Elizabethan cottage at the edge of a golf course is the single outstanding exception, but even this was designed by an out-of-town architect. Downtown was no different. Its single, strong period piece from the 1920's, a colorful Mediterranean Revival movie palace, the Washington Theater, was the creation of a Chicago architect. The buoyant optimism and glowing financial prospects that had raised Quincy's architecture far above the norm for a city its size had

at last run their course, and the city settled down to live with the creations of its past.

Quincy had one last burst of architectural energy left before the advent of what we now regard as the contemporary period. Near the close of the Great Depression, George Behrensmeyer's nephew, also trained at the University of Illinois, unleashed a folio of designs in a pure Moderne Style. Charles Behrensmeyer's early work provided the transition to architecture of contemporary times. The Ernest Chatten house is foremost among examples of this work, but the State Theater and Schemming's clothing store were at one time equally striking designs. Schemming's also had the distinction of introducing custom plywood cabinetry and fluorescent lights to commercial architecture in the city. With these buildings, the historic period of Quincy's architecture comes to an end.

The great richness of Quincy's architectural legacy is in many ways the child of a nineteenth-century optimism that the city would fill whatever boundaries it was given. The immigrant-dominated south side, predominately vernacular in character, expanded in an orderly fashion, its growth keeping pace with the incremental extension of its boundaries to the southeast. But this kind of linear expansion was exceptional. On the east-west downtown streets of the 1840's, again in the north side after the Civil War, and once more in the east end in the 1890's, buildings sprang up in isolation or in small pockets that would not be connected into neighborhoods for many years. The result is that every neighborhood but the south side is anchored by substantial buildings, one or two or even three generations older than those that eventually lined its streets. It is this amazing compression of history, and the rich variety of form and style that comes with it, that elevates Quincy's architectural legacy above scholarly interest into a thing of beauty.

(LEFT AND ABOVE)
John and Ann Wood Mansion
425 South 12th Street

1835

(ABOVE AND INSET)
Lorenzo and Margaret Bull House
1550 Maine Street

1852

(RIGHT)
Charles and Anna Bull House
1651 Maine Street

1855

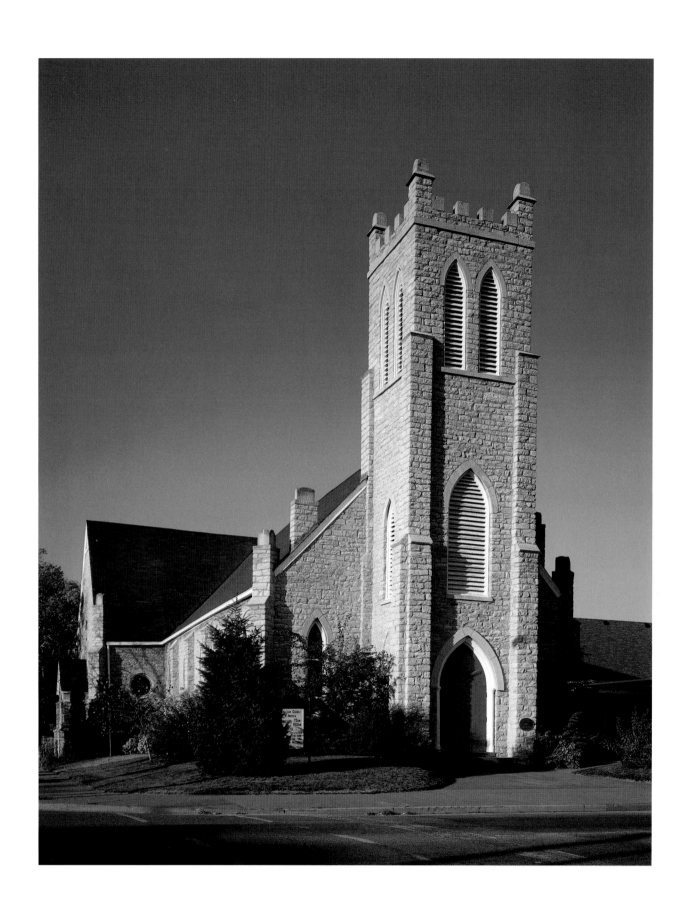

St. John's Episcopal Church
701 Hampshire Street

1852

(ABOVE AND INSET)
Norwood-Morgan-Wells House
421 Jersey Street

1858

Matthew and Electa Finlay House
1617 Hampshire Street

1860

(Above)
Benjamin and Elizabeth Burroughs House
3130 State Street

1865

(Below)
Philip and Fannie Bert House
1475 Hampshire Street

1870

(Previous Pages)
Quincy College
1800 College Avenue

1870

(Above)
Temple B'nai Sholom
427 North 9th Street

1870

Henry and Catharine Dickhut House
1401 Maine Street

c. 1872

Frederick and Leondine Reinecker House
1470 Vermont Street

1872

John and Casper Ruff House
1137-1139 Adams Street

1872

F. W. Jansen Furniture Factory
801 South Front Street

1873

St. Pauli German Evangelical Lutheran Church
927 Monroe Street

1874

(LEFT)
Dricus and Fanny Snitjer House
1469 Maine Street

1876

(ABOVE)
Edward and Fanny Manson House
1636 Maine Street

1876

(BELOW)
William and Alice McFadon House
1637 Hampshire Street

1876

FORUM

GRIFFIN CENTRE

(LEFT)
Ricker National Bank
415 Hampshire Street

1876

(ABOVE)
Salem Evangelical Church
437 South 9th Street

1877

(ABOVE)
James and Maggie Bradshaw House
819 North 5th Street

1878

(BELOW)
Edward and Katherine Pfanschmidt House
205 South 16th Street

1878

C.D. Behrensmeyer Store
1001-1003 State Street

1881

William and Anna Richardson House
1804 Jersey Street

1883

Joanna R. Wallace House
210 South 18th Street

c. 1883

(Left and Above)
St. Francis Solanus Catholic Church
1721 College Avenue

1885

Samuel and Mary Brown House
822 North 6th Street
1886

Headquarters Building
Illinois Soldiers' and Sailors' (now Veterans) Home
1707 North 12th Street

1886

(Previous Pages)
Timothy Rogers Block
119-129 North 6th Street

1886

(Above)
William and Malvina Warfield House
1624 Maine Street

1886

Charles and Emily Williamson House
220 North 16th Street

c. 1886

(LEFT)
William and Mary Bull House
222 South 16th Street
—————
1887

(ABOVE)
Lorenzo and Margaret Bull Carriage House
1515 Jersey Street
—————
1887

De Lafayette and Virginia Musselman House
2203 Maine Street

1887

U.S. Courthouse and Post Office
200 North 8th Street

1887

(ABOVE AND INSET)
Quincy Public Library and Reading Room
332 Maine Street

1888

Ezra and Florence Best House
238 South 12th Street

1889

Anton and Ellen Binkert House
1220 Park Place

1889

(ABOVE)
Blackstone Building
237 North 6th Street

1889

(RIGHT)
Charles and Anna Comstock House
1665 Hampshire Street

c. 1889

(ABOVE)
John and Anna Cruttenden House #1
1200 Park Place

1889

(BELOW)
Albert and Anna Dick House
1102 State Street

1889

Theodore and Ella Poling House
2016 Jersey Street

1890

(ABOVE)
Samuel and Lida Scott House
405 South 24th Street

c. 1890

(BELOW AND ON TITLE PAGE)
Isaac and Ellen Lesem House
1449 Maine Street

1891

70

(ABOVE)
Edward and Matilda Menke House
1206 Park Place

1891

(BELOW)
Henry Arnsman House
1037 South 16th Street

c. 1892

(ABOVE)
Konefes "Spec" Houses
208 and 212 South 12th Street

1892

(INSET)
Konefes "Spec" House
212 South 12th Street

1892

(ABOVE AND INSET)
State Savings Loan and Trust Co.
428 Maine Street

1892

(ABOVE)
"Ivy Wall," Harvey and Anna Chatten House
1838 Jersey Street

1893

(BELOW)
John and Anna Ellis House
1834 Jersey Street

1894

Grant and Olive Irwin House
1656 Maine Street

1894

(ABOVE AND BELOW)
George and Mary Stahl House
300 South 18th Street

1894

John Willis and Helen Gardner House
228 South 18th Street

1895

St. John the Baptist Catholic Church
1019 Cedar Street

1895

William and Ella Dwire House
1621 Vermont Street

c. 1897

William and Mary Figgen House
1605 Hampshire Street

1897

Edward and Elenora Rogers House
1627 Maine Street

c. 1897

Ernest and Clara Wood House
1843 Grove Avenue

1897

"Villa Kathrine," George Metz House
532 Gardner Expressway

1900

Dodd Building
100 North 5th Street

1897

(ABOVE)
Dick Brothers Brewery Office and Brew House
901 and 905 York Street

1901

(INSET)
Dick Brothers Brewery Office
901 York Street

1901

John and Anna Cruttenden House #2
2020 Maine Street
1904

(ABOVE)
George and Sadie Dashwood House
1801 Maine Street

1908

(BELOW)
Paul and Rhoda Gardner House
2325 Maine Street

1908

Otto and Anna Mohrenstecher House
1845 Jersey Street

1908

North Side Boat Club
200 South Front Street

1909

(ABOVE AND INSET)
Charles and Flora Appleton House
2000 Jersey Street

1909

(ABOVE)
Frederick and Anna Wilms House
2084 Maine Street

1910

(BELOW)
George and Sarah Wells House
224 South 20th Street

c. 1911

91

Fredericka Halbach House
129 East Avenue

1912

Ernest Wood Office and Studio
126 North 8th Street

1912

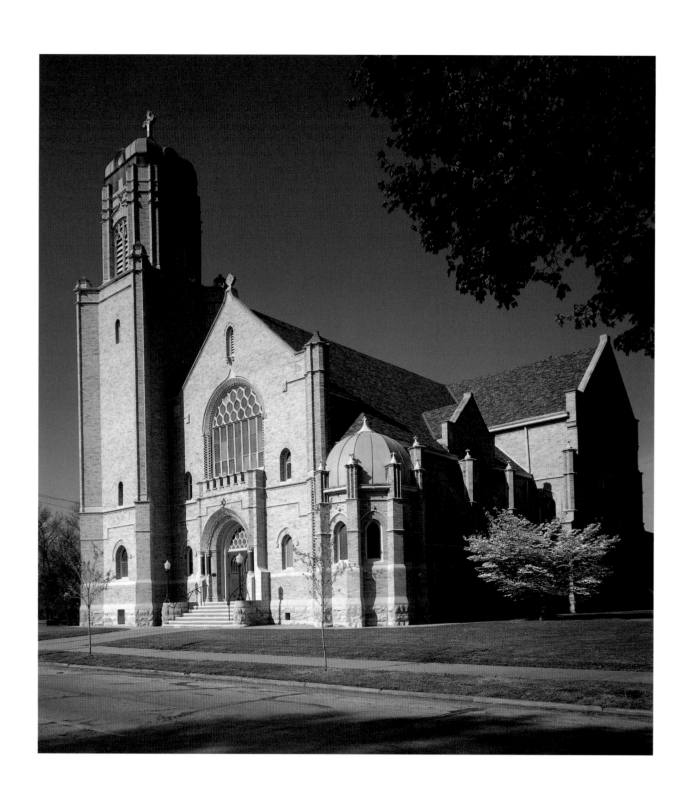

St. Rose of Lima Catholic Church
1009 North 8th Street

1912

(ABOVE AND INSET)
Henry and Flora Bastert House
1850 Jersey Street

1913

(LEFT)
Illinois State Bank Building
531 Hampshire Street

1914

(ABOVE)
Hugh and Effie King House
221 North 24th Street

c. 1914

97

Unitarian Church
1479 Hampshire Street

1914

WHO DARES
TO TEACH
MUST NEVER
CEASE
TO LEARN

Washington School
1401 North 8th Street

1914

(ABOVE)
Carl and Olive Bucklo House
2125 Prairie Avenue

1916

(BELOW)
Martin and Frances Geise House
300 East Avenue

1916

(ABOVE)
John and Mary Reticker House
330 East Avenue

1916

(BELOW)
George and Grace Behrensmeyer House
333 East Avenue

1917

Dewey School
2040 Cherry Street

1917

Washington Park Bandstand and Lincoln-Douglas Plaque
Washington Park

1918, 1936

Henry and Clara Sprick House
2320 York Street
1923

Washington Theater and Offices
425 Hampshire Street

1924

(Left)
Walter and Dorothy Stevenson House
709 South 24th Street

c. 1927

(Above)
Henry and Catherine Finkenhoefer House
1728 Chestnut Street

c. 1928

(PREVIOUS PAGES AND ABOVE)
Quincy Senior High School
100 South 14th Street

1929

Zwick Row
2428-2444 College Avenue

1939

Ernest and Genevieve Chatten House
2336 Oak Street

1939

(PAGE 114)
Dr. Richard and Jane Eells House
415 Jersey Street

1835, 1841, 1854, 1858, 1871

Dr. Richard Eells was the leading abolitionist in Quincy from the late 1830's to his death in 1846. Ensuing owners gradually changed his simple house, one of the first brick structures in Quincy, into a vernacular version of the Italianate Style, to be used for rental purposes. The house is being developed into a museum by the Friends of the Dr. Richard Eells House, which interprets both the abolitionist associations and the structural evolution of the building.

(PAGES 26-27)
John and Ann Wood Mansion
425 South 12th Street

1835-1838, 1864
John Cleaveland, builder

In its early years, every house visible from John Wood's property at the edge of town was made of logs. Originally facing State Street, the mansion was moved across 12th Street in 1864 to clear the approach to Wood's new and even grander octagonal stone mansion, now demolished. This move was accomplished by raising the house up and over Wood's favorite osage orange hedge without damaging it. The early mansion now stands on a busy commercial corner, surrounded by trees and neatly separated from the twentieth century by a picket fence. Listed on the National Register of Historic Places, it is maintained as a house museum by the Historical Society of Quincy and Adams County.

(PAGE 114)
Lloyd and Mercy Morton House
2210 Broadway

1837

Built for a pioneering land developer, the Morton house expressed a builder's attempt at Greek Revival, with its corner pilasters reiterated at either side of the entry vestibule. The side porches were originally open.

(PAGE 114)
Benjamin and Electa Terrel House
2531 Prentiss Avenue

1840, c. 1862

This four-room house, one of Quincy's oldest surviving brick buildings, was originally a dormitory for students at the Mission Institute nearby. In the 1960's, small end-stacks were replaced by a massive central chimney, giving the house the appearance of a colonial cottage.

(PAGE 28)
Lorenzo and Margaret Bull House
1550 Maine Street

1852-1854, 1886

This Italianate house has a distinguished chain of ownership, from prominent merchant and financier Lorenzo Bull to his daughter Elizabeth and her husband, Boulevard and Park Association founder Edward Parker, to the Quincy Park District. The house is now occupied by the Women's City Club, while the carriage house has been converted into the Quincy Art Center.

(PAGE 30)
St. John's Episcopal Church
701 Hampshire Street

1852-1853, 1865, 1879
Charles Howland, architect
Robert Bunce, architect of 1879 addition

St. John's Church is a local architect's simplification of Richard Upjohn's Gothic Revival manner. The church grew in size and interior splendor through much of the nineteenth century, with the most significant addition being a chapel added by Robert Bunce.

(PAGE 114)
Wesley and Susan McCann House
1668 Maine Street

1854, c. 1890

The McCanns built their east end house at the same time as the Bull brothers but on a tiny patch of land and in the old-fashioned Greek Revival Style. The porches and attic dormer are additions from a later period when the neighborhood was finally beginning to fill with houses.

(PAGE 29)
Charles and Anna Bull House
1651 Maine Street

1855-1857, 1876, c. 1922
George Baumann, original builder

Charles and Anna Bull took a bit longer than Charles's brother to erect their Italianate suburban house but gave it a grander air by building with brick and surmounting it with a glazed belvedere visible from the edge of downtown. The three-acre estate included a large carriage house containing not only horses and carriages but also cows, which were pastured a few blocks away.

(PAGE 31)
Norwood-Morgan-Wells House
Joseph and E.J. Norwood, James and Harriet Morgan, Edward and Mary Wells
421 Jersey Street

1858, 1860

Remodeling during the Civil War turned this Italianate house, owned by a succession of wealthy pork packers and financiers, into one of the city's fullest expressions of the style. A large Renaissance Revival gymnasium was added in 1903, shortly after the mansion became Cheerful Home, the first day-care center in Illinois. The mansion is listed on the National Register of Historic Places and now houses the YWCA.

(PAGE 32)
Matthew and Electa Finlay House
1617 Hampshire Street

1860

The Finlay house was one of several between downtown and the east end to sport a cupola just before the Civil War. The Finlays took possession the day Fort Sumter was fired upon. The many gaps between these early Italianate mansions gradually filled with equally grand houses in later styles, creating a large upscale neighborhood.

Dr. Richard and Jane Eells House
415 Jersey Street
1835

Benjamin and Electa Terrel House
2531 Prentiss Avenue
1840

(BUILDING ON LEFT)
Johann Schurmeier Building
729 Maine Street
1866

(BUILDING ON RIGHT)
Hoeckelman Building
735 Maine Street
1894

Lloyd and Mercy Morton House
2210 Broadway
1837

Wesley and Susan McCann House
1668 Maine Street
1854

(PAGE 33)

Benjamin and Elizabeth Burroughs House
3130 State Street

1865

Benjamin Burroughs was unusual for making his fortune before coming to Quincy. He parlayed a strike in the Colorado gold rush into a small fortune, then moved to Adams County to build one of its most richly detailed farmhouses.

(PAGE 114)

Johann Schurmeier Building
729 Maine Street

1866

Quincy embarked on an ambitious building campaign in the aftermath of the Civil War, and this was among its first products. The Schurmeier Building combines the massive scrolled brackets and window hoods of the Italianate Style with delicate fretsaw ornament applied to the frieze between the brackets.

(PAGES 9 AND 118)

David and Casandra Miller House
1477 Maine Street

1867

Built in the hybrid Italianate/Second Empire Style locally popular in the aftermath of the Civil War, the Miller house functioned as a hotel for overflow from the Quincy House downtown. It underwent lavish interior remodeling under Ralph Gardner's ownership in the 1920's.

(PAGE 118)

Union Block (partial)
115 North 4th Street

1867

Washington Square was the particular focus of post-Civil War improvements, and the Union Block, once stretching over half of one side of the square, was the most auspicious new building. The block was divided into seven super bays, with a unified cornice and varying designs for the storefronts.

(PAGE 118)

Conrad Bowe House
935 Payson Avenue

1868

The Bowe house is a picture-perfect example of the "Georgian Plan," which improves on a common vernacular arrangement of four equal-sized rooms, one in each corner, by introducing a central hall lit by a strip of windows surrounding the door.

(PAGE 33)

Philip and Fannie Bert House
1475 Hampshire Street

1870

The Gothic cottage arrived late in Quincy and never achieved much popularity. Perhaps clothing merchant Philip Bert was trying to compete with the Italianate mansions around him by dressing up a humble house with multiple peaked roofs and millwork trim.

(PAGES 34-35)

Quincy College
1800 College Avenue

1870-72, 1894-95, 1897-98, 1910-12
Henry Schenk,
architect of 1872 east wing
Fr. Adrian Wewer, architect of 1895 west
wing and 1898 main building
Br. Anselm Wolff, architect of 1912 chapel
Quincy College, now a university, was built in several increments, mostly in a Germanic version of Gothic Revival. Brother Wolff departed from precedent with a magnificent Romanesque Revival chapel placed at the rear of the main building.

(PAGE 36)

Temple B'nai Sholom
427 North 9th Street

1870

Robert Bunce, architect
The temple was built midway between the residential neighborhood and the workplaces of a thriving north-side Jewish community. Robert Bunce's design incorporates a number of Islamic elements, which seems curiously anachronistic today, though commonplace in synagogue and temple design in the latter half of the nineteenth century.

(PAGE 37)

Henry and Catharine Dickhut House
1401 Maine Street

c. 1872, porches 1886
Built by prominent lawyer Onias Skinner, the house was first occupied by lumber merchant Henry Dickhut and his new wife. Its elaborate porches, with their half-Gothic, half-classical columns, were later alterations that blend well with the original architecture.

(PAGE 38)

Frederick and Leondine Reinecker House
1470 Vermont Street

1872

Frederick Reinecker, builder
The son of a German immigrant builder, Frederick Reinecker became one of the city's most successful builders in his own right. Like most of his residential work, his house for himself was executed to his own design.

(PAGE 39)

John and Casper Ruff House
1137-1139 Adams Street

1872

The Ruff brothers ran one of the city's largest breweries immediately to the east of their double house, while the mansion also lorded it over rows of workers' cottages to the south and west. Most of the money spent on the house went for show; its interiors are starkly simple.

(PAGE 118)

Sarah A. Baker House
327 South 12th Street

1873

Attributed to Robert Bunce, architect
Sarah Baker's mother was the first woman to develop an addition to Quincy. Presumably, this house for Sarah and her younger daughter, Fanny, was built with some of the profits. The quality of its detailing suggests the hand of local architect Robert Bunce.

(PAGE 40)

F. W. Jansen Furniture Factory
801 South Front Street

1873

Robert Bunce, architect
F. W. Jansen and his son were major manufacturers of fine furniture for nearly 50 years. This was their third and largest factory, sold in 1889 to a company that extracted minerals from local stone. In 1901 it passed to Quincy Stove Manufacturing Company, which expanded the building to the south.

(PAGE 41)

St. Pauli German Evangelical
Lutheran Church
927 Monroe Street

1874

Built at a time when Quincy's churches were going Gothic, St. Pauli stubbornly adhered to the round-arched style of the earlier part of the century. Probably inspired by the German neoclassicism familiar to its congregation, it also fit with the periodic American flashes of Romanesque Revival.

(PAGES 8 AND 42)

Dricus and Fanny Snitjer House
1469 Maine Street

1876, 1881

Attributed to John S. McKean, architect
Of Quincy's nineteenth-century architects, John S. McKean had the keenest grasp of accurate stylistic detail, and the Snitjer house is far and away the best residential example of the Second Empire Style in the city. Its swollen roof slopes and iron crestings are particularly noteworthy. Built and first occupied by the Snitjers, by 1882 it became the home of Mathias and Ada Huffman.

(PAGE 43)

Edward and Fanny Manson House
1636 Maine Street

1876

Attributed to Robert Bunce, architect
As the Italianate Style waned in popularity, local builders and architects tended toward a mix of historical and fanciful detailing that defied stylistic classification. The Manson house is typical of these in its use of ornament derived from the famed English arbiter of taste, Charles Eastlake.

(PAGE 43)

William and Alice McFadon House
1637 Hampshire Street

1876, porch late 1880's

The McFadons' humble cottage belied the fortune in financing and real estate speculation garnered by William and his father, John. It was a wedding present from Alice's parents, Charles and Anna Bull. The Gothic adornments belong to a later period when pattern-book alterations achieved brief local popularity.

(PAGE 44)

Ricker National Bank
415 Hampshire Street

1876, 1891

John S. McKean, architect
Harvey Chatten, architect of addition
John S. McKean's fine Second Empire design lost the tower piercing its mansard roof but gained a duplicating addition built 15 years later. The stonework is heavy-handed French Renaissance in form, relieved by incised ornament similar to the fretsaw woodwork of the current Charles Eastlake fashion.

(PAGE 45)

Salem Evangelical Church
437 South 9th Street

1877

John S. McKean, architect
The exterior of Salem Evangelical Church is Victorian Gothic at its most ebullient, with no particular allegiance to the building traditions of its Germanic congregation, while the interior is a wide preaching auditorium contrasting sharply with the long processional space of the Gothic sanctuary of Catholic usage.

(PAGE 46)

James and Maggie Bradshaw House
819 North 5th Street

1878

The Bradshaw house is the high point of pre-Queen Anne eclecticism in Quincy. Built for a preeminent photographer and his wife, it was occupied by Maggie alone after James Bradshaw was committed to an insane asylum in the early 1880's.

(PAGE 46)

Edward and Katherine Pfanschmidt
House
205 South 16th Street

1878, moved 1884

Originally located on the back of the lot where the Warfield house now stands, the Pfanschmidt house was featured in a local house mover's advertisement for 30 years. The house grew a Moorish porch shortly after settling into its new location.

(PAGE 118)

Henry and Josephine Freiburg House
1431 Spring Street

1879

Henry Freiburg was a shoe manufacturer with a penchant for invention. At the height of his success, he put up this quaint suburban cottage, then built a small factory on the grounds. His business soon succumbed to competition with larger manufacturers.

(PAGE 47)

C.D. Behrensmeyer Store
1001-1003 State Street

1881, 1890

A vernacular storefront building was transformed into an exercise in the monumental decor of the Richardsonian Romanesque Style. The weighty effect of the style is belied by the broadly glazed openings of the ground floor.

(PAGE 48)

William and Anna Richardson House
1804 Jersey Street

1883

One of two distinguished examples of the Stick Style in Quincy, the Richardson house is also the oldest in its immediate neighborhood. Its strong horizontal lines anticipated the Shingle Style, which was soon to follow.

(PAGE 49)

Joanna R. Wallace House
210 South 18th Street

c. 1883

Mrs. Wallace's house was among the first in the city to show the simplifying influence the Queen Anne Style had at its inception, while it retains many of the eccentricities (like a window in the chimney) common to eclectic pattern-book designs.

(PAGES 50-51)

St. Francis Solanus Catholic Church
1721 College Avenue

1885-1886

Fr. Adrian Wewer, architect
Father Wewer designed nearly all of the Catholic churches in Quincy and the surrounding region between his arrival in 1862 and his retirement from architectural practice around 1898. St. Francis Solanus is the most complete surviving example of his work in the city.

(PAGE 52)
Samuel and Mary Brown House
822 North 6th Street

1886

Attributed to Harvey Chatten, architect
Harvey Chatten's early Queen Anne designs were almost devoid of classical ornament or millwork; instead they relied on bold geometrical patterns that could easily be produced on the site by a skilled stonemason or carpenter.

(PAGE 53)
Headquarters Building
Illinois Soldiers' and Sailors'
(now Veterans) Home
1707 North 12th Street

1886

Smith M. Randolph, architect
The Gothic fortress that Smith Randolph designed as the main headquarters building has lost its upper story but remains an elemental force. The Quincy location of the state Soldiers' and Sailors' Home was a great coup for the city, achieved largely because of the donation of land by a private estate.

(PAGES 54-55)
Timothy Rogers Block
119-129 North 6th Street

1886, 1889

Harvey Chatten, architect
Designed initially as an upgrading of an existing storefront row, the Rogers Block was Harvey Chatten's first opportunity at extended commercial design. The bow fronts of the upper stories give the buildings a strong residential feel, a sense that is increased by decoratively incised entries at the sidewalk level.

(PAGE 56)
William and Malvina Warfield House
1624 Maine Street

1886

J. Lyman Silsbee, architect
The Warfield house was the first of several Quincy commissions for prominent Chicago architect J. Lyman Silsbee. The stone was imported from Minnesota, while the decorative terra cotta ornament was molded and fired near Chicago. The house is listed on the National Register of Historic Places.

(PAGE 57)
Charles and Emily Williamson House
220 North 16th Street

c. 1886

Initially located on a tiny lot on Hampshire Street, this engaging Stick Style house was pivoted on one of its rear corners onto an equally tiny lot on the side street around 1920. Its striking verticality perfectly suits the restricted lots it has occupied.

(PAGE 58)
William and Mary Bull House
222 South 16th Street

1887

J. Lyman Silsbee, architect
William and Mary Bull were on an extended honeymoon while William's father, Lorenzo, had this massive Shingle Style house built for them across Jersey Street. Frank Lloyd Wright and George Maher worked for J. Lyman Silsbee while the house was being designed, fueling modern speculation that one or both Prairie School architects had a hand in its detailing.

(PAGE 59)
Lorenzo and Margaret Bull Carriage House
1515 Jersey Street

1887

J. Lyman Silsbee, architect
While he was having his house partially updated, Lorenzo Bull retained J. Lyman Silsbee to design a new carriage house in an eclectic style. Modern conversion of the building to the Art Barn and then the Quincy Art Center has not altered the vivid pictorialism of the tower and gables.

(PAGE 60)
De Lafayette and Virginia Musselman House
2203 Maine Street

1887-1889

D. L. Musselman presided over Gem City Business College, which became the largest commercial college in the Midwest. The architect of his house is unknown, though it may have been John Batschy, who would soon design the monumental new headquarters of the college.

(PAGE 122)
Newcomb Hotel
400 Maine Street

1887-1888

Isaac Taylor, architect
Chicago architect J. Lyman Silsbee was originally retained to design this luxury hotel, but his plans proved too expensive to execute. Calling in prominent St. Louis architect Isaac Taylor produced a building that is predominantly classical in tone though mildly Romanesque in detail.

(PAGE 61)
U.S. Courthouse and Post Office
200 North 8th Street

1887, 1911, 1937

Office of the Supervising Architect of the U.S. Treasury
Design under James G. Hill, construction detail under Mifflin E. Bell
The style of the building probably passed for French Renaissance, though Mifflin Bell's detailing also applied some of the fanciful variations of the Second Empire. Additions over a 50-year period were carefully matched in material, and approximately matched in style, to original construction. The building is listed on the National Register of Historic Places.

(PAGE 62)
Quincy Public Library and Reading Room
332 Maine Street

1888-1889

Patton and Fisher, architects
Chicago architects Patton and Fisher followed H. H. Richardson's lead in designing a number of small Romanesque civic buildings for mid-sized communities. The library was housed below, while the reading room stretched beneath the wood-vaulted ceiling of the second floor. The building is now occupied by the Gardner Museum of Architecture & Design.

David and Casandra Miller House
1477 Maine Street
1867

Sarah A. Baker House
327 South 12th Street
1873

Union Block (partial)
115 North 4th Street
1867

Conrad Bowe House
935 Payson Avenue
1868

Henry and Josephine Freiburg House
1431 Spring Street
1879

(PAGE 63)

Ezra and Florence Best House
238 South 12th Street

1889

John Batschy, architect

Built the same year as the opening of Park Place across the street, the Best house also came from the drawing boards of Park Place's chief architect in its early years, John Batschy. It approximates the Richardsonian Romanesque Style, but with several Queen Anne holdovers.

(PAGE 63)

Anton and Ellen Binkert House
1220 Park Place

1889

Anton Binkert was John Cruttenden's partner in the development of Park Place. His own house was designed with a style and taste that were remarkably conservative for their time and place, recalling the eclecticism of the late 1870's rather than the grand manner of the current high styles.

(PAGE 64)

Blackstone Building
237 North 6th Street

1889

The Richardsonian Romanesque Style was often used to provide a dramatic entry arch or enclosure without impinging on the simpler character of the rest of the building. Limestone blocks lining the entry bay of the Blackstone Building appear to support great weight, though they are only a facing on brick.

(PAGE 65)

Charles and Anna Comstock House
1665 Hampshire Street

c. 1889

Harvey Chatten, architect

The Comstock house is the most spectacular of a number of eclectic designs in the neighborhood, most of which have strong affinities with popular pattern-book plans; in this case, the architect of record was rising local talent Harvey Chatten.

(PAGE 66)

John and Anna Cruttenden House #1
1200 Park Place

1889

John Batschy, architect

Cruttenden was one of the two developers of Park Place, the only nineteenth-century covenanted neighborhood in Quincy. His house, prominently located at the western entry, was a showpiece of the new development as well as of late Queen Anne eclecticism.

(PAGE 66)

Albert and Anna Dick House
1102 State Street

1889

John Batschy, architect

The Dick Brothers Brewery was still going strong when the second generation built their houses, as evidenced by Albert's house in his father, Matthew's, subdivision. The design has many similarities with John Cruttenden's house on Park Place just three blocks away.

(PAGE 122)

Trapp Row
303-321 South 10th Street

1889

The shotgun cottage was a popular type for speculative builders, as it could be squeezed onto a 30-foot lot. Though located near the Dick Brothers Brewery, Trapp Row housed occupants of varied trades.

(PAGE 67)

Theodore and Ella Poling House
2016 Jersey Street

1890-1891

Harvey Chatten, architect

In 1889, Theodore Poling joined with several other developers to create the city's first "garden" addition, whose streets followed the terrain in a winding fashion. Poling's own house was the obvious centerpiece of the addition and a masterpiece in the Richardsonian Romanesque Style.

(PAGES 68-69)

Richard and Anna Newcomb House
1601 Maine Street

1890-1891

Harvey Chatten, architect

At the height of Quincy's building boom, paper manufacturer Richard Newcomb replaced his Italianate house with an extraordinary complex essay in the Richardsonian Romanesque Style. The interiors alternate between lavish Romanesque Revival spaces and simpler rooms with classical decor. Now the home of The Quincy Museum, the property is listed on the National Register of Historic Places.

(PAGE 70)

Samuel and Lida Scott House
405 South 24th Street

c. 1890

Though one of the most striking residential designs in a city filled with remarkable architecture, the origin and even precise year of the Scott house are unknown. The house combines classical elements with the long, low slopes of the Shingle Style.

(PAGE 70)

Isaac and Ellen Lesem House
1449 Maine Street

1891, porch c. 1900
Harvey Chatten, architect

Isaac Lesem bought this house on the occasion of his second marriage. As owner of a thriving dry goods business, he could well afford its congeries of Queen Anne, Moorish, and Jacobean "features." Small porches were replaced by a neoclassical veranda at the turn of the century.

(PAGE 71)

Edward and Matilda Menke House
1206 Park Place

1891

John Batschy, architect

The Menke house was among the earliest to join the houses of the developers in the Park Place addition. Though the Menke design lacks the overall force of Cruttenden's, it holds just as many surprises, such as a giant carved cartouche in the spandrel between the first- and second-floor windows.

(PAGE 71)
Henry Arnsman House
1037 South 16th Street

c. 1892

Henry Arnsman built his house at the edge of the old Reichert farm, in a section of Melrose Township that was gradually being absorbed into the city. In form and plan, it could have been designed 30 years earlier; only its masonry detailing gives away its late date.

(PAGE 72)
Konefes "Spec" Houses
208 and 212 South 12th Street

1892
J. H. Konefes and Son, builders

These houses, built on speculation, went up while nearby Park Place was starting to fill, perhaps as advertisement of what J. H. Konefes could do. They combine intricate brickwork with stock ornamental brick and terra cotta made by the Hydraulic Press Brick Company in St. Louis.

(PAGE 73)
State Savings Loan and Trust Co.
428 Maine Street

1892, 1906
Patton and Fisher, architects
Ernest M. Wood, architect of addition

No money was spared on the exterior or interior of this building, the final great business owned and managed by the Bull brothers. Its granite facings, massive wood and wrought-iron doors, and ornamental plasterwork are unique in Quincy. Wood's addition is a near-perfect match of the original. The property is listed on the National Register of Historic Places.

(PAGE 74)
"Ivy Wall," Harvey and
Anna Chatten House
1838 Jersey Street

1893
Harvey Chatten, architect

Harvey Chatten must have been particularly proud of the design for his own house, as he submitted it for publication in the *Inland Architect.* The picturesque complexities of its street facade are opposed to the dramatic sweep of its ivy-clad east side gable.

(PAGE 74)
John and Anna Ellis House
1834 Jersey Street

1894
Harvey Chatten, architect

This dramatic Queen Anne house was built for the family of *Quincy Whig* president John Ellis. It forms a striking companion to Harvey Chatten's own house; the scallop embedded in the gable is a particularly compelling feature.

(PAGE 114)
Hoeckelman Building
735 Maine Street

1894
Frank Tubbesing, architect

The Hoeckelman Building was an unusual departure for Frank Tubbesing, who usually worked with a small palette of materials. The foundation is off-buff Mankato stone from Minnesota, the Maine Street facade is gray Berean sandstone from Ohio, and the walls are pressed and specialty brick from St. Louis.

(PAGE 75)
Grant and Olive Irwin House
1656 Maine Street

1894, addition c. 1921
John Batschy, architect
Addition attributed to Ernest M. Wood,
architect

The Irwin house shows how easily the Richardsonian Romanesque Style could be flattened out into just one more way of dressing up the surfaces of a Queen Anne house. The richness of the gable decoration contrasts sharply with the rectilinear simplicity of the Craftsman additions at front and rear.

(PAGE 76)
George and Mary Stahl House
300 South 18th Street

1894
Harvey Chatten, architect

George Stahl made his fortune inventing and manufacturing chicken incubators. His house is a textbook example of Queen Anne Style in the final, classicizing mode that would form a bridge to popular versions of Colonial Revival at the turn of the century.

(PAGE 77)
John Willis and Helen Gardner House
228 South 18th Street

1895
Harvey Chatten, architect

In this deceptively large house for the J. W. Gardner family, whose fortune was based on the patent and manufacture of steam engine governors, Harvey Chatten took one last fond look back to the mix of Queen Anne and Shingle styles that had served him so well in the early 1890's.

(PAGE 78)
St. John the Baptist Catholic Church
1019 Cedar Street

1895-1898
Fr. Joseph A. Still and Ferdinand Schenk,
joint architects

A faltering economy with few wealthy parishioners forced St. John the Baptist Church to fall back on the architectural skills of its own priest. Fortunately he was aided by one of the Schenk brothers, all master craftsmen. The exterior borrows freely from a variety of French and English Romanesque sources.

(PAGE 79)
William and Ella Dwire House
1621 Vermont Street

c. 1897
Attributed to Ernest M. Wood, architect

Ernest Wood was the only local architect who rode the Tudor Revival into the twentieth century. Stylistically, the Dwire house could have been designed 10 years later, for it has all the earmarks of an overblown Craftsman cottage.

(PAGE 80)
William and Mary Figgen House
1605 Hampshire Street

1897, porte cochere c. 1919
George H. Behrensmeyer, architect

George Behrensmeyer tendered his Figgen house design for state certification as an architect. Like the Schmidt house of the previous year, it applies refined decorative touches to a boldly handled version of the Queen Anne Style.

(PAGE 81)
Edward and Elenora Rogers House
1627 Maine Street

c. 1897

The Richardsonian Romanesque house is given a cheery air by a colorful Mankato limestone from Minnesota and unusually delicate ornament. Its odd site, squeezed between two mansions, is the result of the Rogers' desperate purchase of land off the Distin parcel at $1,000 a front-foot so that they could live on this part of Maine Street.

(PAGE 82)
Ernest and Clara Wood House
1843 Grove Avenue

1897, 1907, 1915
Ernest M. Wood, architect

Little of Ernest Wood's early work has been identified. This house for his own family is Queen Anne in inspiration, though its Tudor detailing could easily be adapted to the more rectilinear forms of the Craftsman Style that would follow.

(PAGE 83)
"Villa Kathrine," George Metz House
532 Gardner Expressway

1900-1901
George H. Behrensmeyer, architect

George Metz and his house were one-of-a-kind. The eccentric bachelor toured North Africa and Spain for inspiration, then hired a young local architect to put his ideas into a workable design. The house is undergoing restoration as a house museum while doubling as the local tourism information center. It is listed on the National Register of Historic Places.

(PAGE 84)
Dodd Building
100 North 5th Street

1897, 1923
Ernest M. Wood, architect

The tallest building on the square since its erection, the Dodd Building is a reserved statement of neoclassicism in a commercial mode; segmental bow fronts provide the only relief for the walls, while a sheet metal cornice is fleshed out with finely detailed modillions.

(PAGE 122)
Milton Waide Photographic Studio
130 North 8th Street

1900
Ernest M. Wood, architect

The Waide Studio marked an important breakthrough in Ernest Wood's evolution as an architect. After several years of attaching Tudoresque features to late Victorian houses, he finally let the last touches of the Queen Anne Style slip away and poured his Tudor Revival ideas into a pure Craftsman mold. The building is listed on the National Register of Historic Places.

(PAGE 85)
Office and Brew House
901 and 905 York Street

1901

After nearly 40 years of business on the south side of York Street, Dick Brothers Brewery moved its offices and its main brewing operation into new facilities across the street. In the new office building, overscaled tin cornice work applies a hint of the Renaissance to a late Queen Anne design.

Brewery buildings were generally the province of architects who specialized in them; these brewery houses were done by an unidentified St. Louis firm. Though the new brewery houses are primarily functional in character, the masonry patterns of their walls probably derive from popular picture books of brickwork in northern Italy.

(PAGE 86)
John and Anna Cruttenden House #2
2020 Maine Street

1904
Ernest M. Wood, architect

When John Cruttenden moved out of his Park Place subdivision, he chose a totally different type of house, rejecting the fanciful masonry of the Queen Anne at its most eclectic for the simple classical rigors of a frame Colonial Revival.

(PAGE 87)
George and Sadie Dashwood House
1801 Maine Street

1908
George H. Behrensmeyer, architect

One of the oldest houses in the east end was moved off this lot to accommodate a neoclassical design with a giant order portico. Probably marked as a Colonial Revival design, it is actually an amalgam of classical devices with largely Craftsman interiors.

(PAGE 87)
Paul and Rhoda Gardner House
2325 Maine Street

1908
Harvey Chatten, architect

The sweeping diagonal lines of the roof betray Harvey Chatten's continued attachment to the Shingle Style, but the purposely unmatched and mottled brick and the simple, structural ornament show that he was edging his way toward a Craftsman sensibility.

(PAGE 88)
Otto and Anna Mohrenstecher House
1845 Jersey Street

1908, 1930
Harvey Chatten, architect
Ernest M. Wood, architect of additions

The Mohrenstecher house exudes the prosperous but quiet respectability of the successful department store merchant who occupied it. Ernest Wood's additions, a car porch and rear wing, meld seamlessly into the original design.

(PAGE 89)
North Side Boat Club
200 South Front Street

1909
Martin J. Geise, architect

As the steamboat era passed, a number of private boat clubs sprang up along the river. The North Side Boat Club had the only clubhouse with architectural pretensions, a stunning Baroque front that wrapped just enough of the sides to give the illusion of a thoroughgoing high-style building.

Newcomb Hotel
400 Maine Street

1887

Milton Waide Photographic Studio
130 North 8th Street

1900

Trapp Row
303-321 South 10th Street

1889

South Park Pavilion
South Park

1917

(PAGE 90)
Charles and Flora Appleton House
2000 Jersey Street

1909
Ernest M. Wood, architect

In the Appleton house, Ernest Wood pushed the Colonial Revival as far in the Craftsman direction as it would go without losing the requisite sense of symmetry and a semblance of neoclassical detailing. The native stone masonry work of the house is particularly fine.

(PAGE 91)
Frederick and Anna Wilms House
2084 Maine Street

1910

The Wilms house is as striking for its austerity as for the wealth of its ornamental program. Built for the president of Wabash Coal Company, it brings the English country house of the early eighteenth century up to date and onto a much-traveled city street.

(PAGE 91)
George and Sarah Wells House
224 South 20th Street

c. 1911
Harvey Chatten, architect

George Wells was close to retirement when he hired Harvey Chatten to plan a new house for him. The resulting design has some of the feel of an English manor from the approaching drive, but the interior is distinctly modern and American in its open axial spaces, suited to accommodating large receptions.

(PAGE 92)
Fredericka Halbach House
129 East Avenue

1912
Ernest M. Wood, architect

Frank Lloyd Wright's influence crept slowly into Quincy, largely through the agency of Ernest Wood. This is Wood's most effective local residential essay in the Prairie School manner, though the design is compromised by the use of sash rather than casement windows.

(PAGE 93)
Ernest Wood Office and Studio
126 North 8th Street

1912
Ernest M. Wood, architect

Ernest Wood's purest Prairie School residences were all constructed for clients in outlying towns. In his hometown, only his place of work showed the depth of his reverence for Frank Lloyd Wright. Its finest space is a small office overlooking the street and heated (at least figuratively) by a central fireplace. The building is listed on the National Register of Historic Places.

(PAGE 94)
St. Rose of Lima Catholic Church
1009 North 8th Street

1912
George H. Behrensmeyer, architect

In designing this north-side church, George Behrensmeyer departed from the familiar Gothic territory of the city's other Catholic churches to embrace a bit of the Romanesque, a bit of the Gothic, and a bit of the Renaissance, holding it all together with a tower that is largely Baroque in inspiration.

(PAGE 95)
Henry and Flora Bastert House
1850 Jersey Street

1913
George H. Behrensmeyer, architect

Never shy about creating monumental effects, George Behrensmeyer designed a house for the Basterts in which each element of the exterior seems to express some of the qualities of the native gray limestone. Curiously, the interior casework is nearly identical to that of his houses in a neoclassical vein.

(PAGE 96)
Illinois State Bank Building
531 Hampshire Street

1914
Martin J. Geise, architect

This was the first building in Quincy to be clad entirely in terra cotta. Martin Geise chose a stock pattern, probably of Chicago origin. The material, particularly if coated with a hard glaze, was believed to have a life as long as hard-burned brick, which it resembled in composition.

(PAGE 97)
Hugh and Effie King House
221 North 24th Street

c. 1914

Quincy bungalows on the whole possessed little in the way of the attached garden structures that distinguished so many of their California peers. This one is exceptional for its elaborate pergola as well as the high quality of its masonry work.

(PAGE 98)
Unitarian Church
1479 Hampshire Street

1914
Harvey Chatten, architect

Harvey Chatten's last church design shows him still struggling to let go of his Queen Anne past. The building is predominately Craftsman in style, but much of its vivid pictorial effect is created by such late Victorian details as the corner turrets and witch's hat that crown the tower.

(PAGE 99)
Washington School
1401 North 8th Street

1914
Ernest M. Wood, architect

The plan of Ernest Wood's design for Washington School drew considerable critical attention because it expressed a growing public concern for fire safety by keeping all students on a single floor. Today its chief interest is its stunning visual layout, which owes an obvious debt to the Prairie School.

(PAGE 100)
Carl and Olive Bucklo House
2125 Prairie Avenue

1916

The Bucklo house has the aspect of a Craftsman bungalow, though it outreaches the humble proportions of that building type. Tudor Revival details, such as a side window headed with a low Gothic arch, are inserted into a design that seems in other respects to be aggressively assertive of the new, anti-historic idiom.

(PAGE 100)
Martin and Frances Geise House
300 East Avenue

1916
Martin J. Geise, architect

Martin Geise's design for his own family's house owes a considerable debt to the Prairie School, though it has more affinity with such conservative Frank Lloyd Wright associates as Talmadge and Watson than it does with Wright himself. It is also one of the largest houses Geise was to design.

(PAGE 101)

John and Mary Reticker House
330 East Avenue

1916
Martin J. Geise, architect

The design of the Reticker house was based on a "concrete bungalow" plan developed by Walter Burley Griffin, at one time Frank Lloyd Wright's chief assistant. The grouping of second-story windows at the corners is a distinctive Griffin feature.

(PAGE 101)

George and Grace Behrensmeyer House
333 East Avenue

1917
George H. Behrensmeyer, architect

George Behrensmeyer's house for his family is without question his finest piece of residential design. Though Prairie School in general character, it also expresses Behrensmeyer's distinctive gift for handling weighty materials and monumental volumes without loss of pictorial quality or human scale.

(PAGE 102)

Dewey School
2040 Cherry Street

1917
George H. Behrensmeyer, architect

Most of George Behrensmeyer's schools realized some comfortable variant of the popular Collegiate Gothic Style, but this one strikes out into the less populous territory explored by Chicago architect Dwight Perkins, who proved that Frank Lloyd Wright's principles could be economically applied to large institutional buildings.

(PAGE 122)

South Park Pavilion
South Park

1917
George H. Behrensmeyer, architect

George Behrensmeyer's pavilion has come to symbolize the controlled wildness of South Park. Its horizontal form and strong overhangs provide a convincing image of shelter while contrasting dramatically with the upward-thrusting grove of trees around it.

(PAGE 103)

Washington Park Bandstand and
Lincoln-Douglas Plaque
Washington Park

1918, 1936
Harvey Chatten, architect

Harvey Chatten's design of the Washington Park bandstand was instantly lauded for its artistic merit, but well-placed misgivings about its acoustics delayed construction for two years. The private donation of a citizen who insisted on controlling the use of his money finally broke the deadlock. Nearby, a bronze relief by renowned Chicago sculptor Lorado Taft is the only public memorial of the celebrated 1858 debates that portrays Douglas as well as Lincoln.

(PAGE 104)

Henry and Clara Sprick House
2320 York Street

1923
George H. Behrensmeyer, architect

In the Sprick house, George Behrensmeyer melded the English Arts and Crafts Movement with the Prairie School. Even the art glass vacillates between the two parents, with some echoing English antecedents and others following Frank Lloyd Wright's inspiration.

(PAGE 105)

Washington Theater and Offices
425 Hampshire Street

1924, 1937
E. P. Rupert, architect

In the 1920's, stage and movie theater buildings were an important venue for gaudy facades stylistically matched to lavish interiors. A number of Chicago architects made a specialty of it. E. P. Rupert's design is in an eclectic "Mediterranean" mode with sprinklings of Chicago-based terra cotta patterns.

(PAGE 106)

Walter and Dorothy Stevenson House
709 South 24th Street

c. 1927

A stagnant economy in the 1920's kept the picturesque, pseudo-medieval English cottages that took the country's suburbs by storm from making very deep inroads in Quincy. The Stevenson house, said to be designed by a Milwaukee architect, is the most outstanding local example of the fashion.

(PAGE 107)

Henry and Catherine Finkenhoefer House
1728 Chestnut Street

c. 1928

An unknown architect designed this bungalow, Quincy's last tribute to the Prairie School. The geometrical glazing of the gable peak derives from the work of Frank Lloyd Wright's followers in the early 1910's; here it elevates to artistic stature an otherwise unremarkable design.

(PAGES 108-110)

Quincy Senior High School
100 South 14th Street

1929-1931
James Chubb, architect
Behrensmeyer and Hafner, associate
architects

The planning and engineering of the high school came from James Chubb's office in Chicago, while Behrensmeyer and Hafner designed much of the detailing. A conventional Collegiate Gothic skin covers a number of striking art deco interiors, the most important of which is a central auditorium that seats 2,012 people. The building now serves as the Quincy Junior High School.

(PAGE 111)

Zwick Row
2428-2444 College Avenue

1939
Bauhaus and Zwick, builders

This row of five spectacular houses captures the Moderne Style in several moods: hard-edged and round-cornered, monumental and flimsy, unadorned and aggressively textured, unified and loosely connected. Whether the builders had architectural assistance has not been determined.

(PAGE 112)

Ernest and Genevieve Chatten House
2336 Oak Street

1939
Charles Behrensmeyer, architect

In 1938 and 1939, local architect Charles Behrensmeyer produced a number of distinguished Moderne designs in Quincy. The Chatten house was his most original statement, wrapping a free-flowing geometry with a taut skin of cement and embellishing it with the newest industrial materials.

Quincy on the Mississippi River

Adams County Courthouse, *14, 18, 23*
Adams School, *17*
Appleton House, Charles and Flora, *123*
Architechnics, Inc., *5*
Arnsman House, Henry, *120*
Art Barn, *117*
Baker House, Sarah A., *115*
Baker, Fanny, *115*
Baker, James T., *14*
Bangs, Mr., *15*
Barnard, Mariann, *5*
Bastert House, Henry and Flora, *123*
Batschy, John, *24, 117, 119, 120*
Bauhaus and Zwick, *124*
Baumann, George, *21, 113*
Behrensmeyer and Hafner, *124*
Behrensmeyer House, George and Grace, *124*
Behrensmeyer, C. D., Store, *116*
Behrensmeyer, Charles, *25, 124*
Behrensmeyer, George H., *24, 25, 121, 123, 124*
Bell, Mifflin E., *117*
Bert House, Philip and Fannie, *115*
Bert, Philip, *115*
Best House, Ezra and Florence, *119*
Binkert House, Anton and Ellen, *119*
Blackstone Building, *119*
Bonansinga, Joe, *5*
Boscobel, *14*
Boulevard and Park Association, *113*
Bowe House, Conrad, *115*
Bradshaw House, James and Maggie, *116*
Bradshaw, James, *116*
Bradshaw, Maggie, *116*
Brinkman, Nancy, *5*
Broemmel, Reaugh, *5*
Brown House, Samuel and Mary, *117*
Browning, Orville H., *14, 18*
Bucklo House, Carl and Olive, *123*
Buerkin and Kaempen, *15*
Bull brothers, *21, 113, 120*
Bull Carriage House, Lorenzo and Margaret, *117*
Bull House, Charles and Anna, *113*
Bull House, Lorenzo and Margaret, *113*
Bull House, William and Mary, *117*
Bull, Charles Henry, *14, 21*
Bull, Lorenzo, *14, 21, 23, 113, 117*
Bull, William, *23*
Bunce, Robert, *22, 23, 24, 113, 115, 116*
Burnham and Root, *23*
Burnham, D. H., and Company, *23*
Burns, Clarisse, *5*
Burns, Marilyn, *5*
Burroughs House, Benjamin and Elizabeth, *115*
Burroughs, Benjamin, *115*
Calftown, *14*
Celebration, Florida, *17*

Cervon, Mr. and Mrs. Lawrence J., *5*
Chamber of Commerce, *24*
Chatten House, Ernest and Genevieve, *124*
Chatten House, Harvey and Anna, *120*
Chatten, Ernest, *25*
Chatten, Harvey, *22, 23, 24, 116, 117, 119, 121, 123, 124, 120*
Cheerful Home, *113*
Chicago, Burlington and Quincy Railroad Depot, *14, 19, 23, 25*
Chubb, James, *124*
Civil War, *18, 21, 22, 25, 113, 115*
Cleaveland, John, *113*
Cleek, Mrs. Patricia Gardner, *5*
Coldwell Banker/Mays Real Estate, Inc., *5*
Coleman Motor Company, Inc., *5*
Comstock House, Charles and Anna, *119*
Congregational Church, *14*
Conover, Joe, *5*
Cray, Marcia, *5*
Crossland, Dr. and Mrs. Merle F., *5*
Cruttenden House #1, John and Anna, *119*
Cruttenden House #2, John and Anna, *121*
Dashwood House, George and Sadie, *121*
DeGreeff, Louis, *5*
Dewey School, *124*
Dick Brothers Brewery Office and Brew House, *121*
Dick Brothers Brewery, *119*
Dick brothers, *15*
Dick House, Albert and Anna, *119*
Dick, Matthew, *119*
Dickhut House, Henry and Catharine, *115*
Dickhut, Henry, *115*
Dodd Building, *121*
Douglas, Stephen A., *14, 18, 124*
Dwire House, William and Ella, *120*
Dwyer, Rob, *5*
East End Historic District, *17*
Eastlake, Charles, *116*
Edgewood Drive, *17*
Eells House, Dr. Richard and Jane, *113*
Eells, Dr. Richard, *14, 113*
Ellis House, John and Anna, *120*
Ellis, John, *120*
Figgen House, William and Mary, *121*
Finkenhoefer House, Henry and Catherine, *124*
Finlay House, Matthew and Electa, *113*
First Presbyterian Church, *22*
Fisher brothers, *15*
Fort Sumter, *113*
Franklin School, *23*
Freiburg House, Henry and Josephine, *116*
Freiburg, Henry, *116*
Friends of the Dr. Richard Eells House, *5, 113*
Gardner Denver Machinery Inc., *5*
Gardner House, John Willis and Helen, *120*
Gardner House, P. H., *24*

Gardner House, Paul and Rhoda, *121*
Gardner Museum of Architecture & Design, *5, 117*
Gardner, J. W., *120*
Gardner, Ralph, *115*
Gardner, Robert, *15*
Gardner-Denver Company, *15*
Garnsey, George, *23*
Geise House, Martin and Frances, *123*
Geise, Martin J., *22-23, 24, 121, 123, 124*
Gem City Business College, *24, 117*
Georgian Plan, *115*
German Village Society, *5*
Germann, Philip, *5*
Great Depression, *19, 25*
Griffin, Walter Burley, *124*
Guardtree Limited/Quincy Development Center, *5*
Halbach House, Fredericka, *123*
Hansen-Spear Funeral Directors, Ltd., *5*
Hauworth, William, *21*
Headquarters Building Illinois Soldiers' and Sailors' Home (now Veterans), *117*
Herring Press, *5, 128*
Hill, James A., *117*
Historical Society of Quincy and Adams County, *5, 20, 113*
Hoeckelman Building, *120*
Hoener, Doris, *5*
Holliday, William and Susan P., *5*
Howland, Charles, *113*
Huffman, Mathias and Ada, *116*
Hydraulic Press Brick Company, *120*
Illinois State Bank Building, *123*
Illustrated Weekly, *19*
Inland Architect, *120*
Irwin House, Grant and Olive, *120*
Irwin, George M., *5*
Ivy Wall, *120*
Jackson, Marion Gardner Arts Fund, *5*
Jackson, Marion Gardner Charitable Trust, *5*
Jansen, F. W., Furniture Factory, *115*
Jersey Street, *17, 117*
John's Square, *18, 20, 22*
Keyes, Willard, *18*
KHQA TV, *5*
King House, Hugh and Effie, *123*
Knapheide Manufacturing Co., The, *5*
Konefes "Spec" Houses, *120*
Konefes and Son, J.H., *120*
Landrum, Carl, *5, 15, 128*
Larkworthy, William, *15*
Larson, Paul Clifford, *5, 18, 128*
Lawndale, *24*
Lesem House, Isaac and Ellen, *23, 119*
Leslie, Frank, *19*
Lincoln, Abraham, *14, 124*
Lincoln-Douglas Debate of 1858, *22*
Lincoln-Douglas Plaque, *124*

Lindsay, Mrs. A. O., Jr., 5
Link, Theodore, 19
Little River Development Co., 5
Littlefield, Eaton, 15, 21
Maher, George, 24, 117
Manson House, Edward and Fanny, 116
Mason, Carol, 5
Mays, Robert A., 5
McCann House, Wesley and Susan, 113
McFadon House, William and Alice, 116
McFadon, Alice, 116
McFadon, William, 116
McKean, John S., 18, 22, 116
McNay, Richard and Patti, 5
Melrose Township, 120
Menke House, Edward and Matilda, 119
Metz House, George, 84, 121
Miller House, David and Casandra, 9, 115, 118
Miller, David W., 14
Mission Institute, 113
Mississippi River, 14, 18, 19, 21
Mohrenstecher House, Otto and Anna, 121
Morgan, James and Harriet, 113
Morton House, Lloyd and Mercy, 113
Morton, Lloyd and Mercy, 20
Musselman, D. L., 117
Musselman House, De Lafayette and Virginia, 117
National Register districts, 20
National Register of Historic Places, 113, 117, 119, 120, 121, 123
Newcomb Hotel, 117
Newcomb House, Richard and Anna, 119
Newcomb, Richard F., 14, 24
North Fifth Street, 17
North Side Boat Club, 121
Norwood, Joseph and E. J., 113
Norwood-Morgan-Wells House, 113
Oakley, Peter A., 5
Octagon House, 20
Office of the Supervising Architect of the U.S. Treasury, 117
Ohio River, 14
Opera House, 14
Paben, Mary Catherine, 5
Palliser, George, 23
Park Place subdivision, 17, 24, 119, 121
Parker, Edward, 113
Parker, Elizabeth Bull, 113
Patton and Fisher, 23, 117, 120
Paxton, Pattie, 5
Payne, Richard, 5, 128
Perkins, Dwight, 124
Pfanschmidt House, Edward and Katherine, 116
Pierson, Ridgely, 5
Poling House, Theodore and Ella, 119
Poling, Theodore C., 14
Presbyterian Church, 14
Project Steering Committee, 5
Quincy Art Center, 5, 113, 117
Quincy City Hall, 14
Quincy College, 115

Quincy Foundation, 5
Quincy Herald-Whig, The, 5
Quincy Senior High School, 124
Quincy House, 14, 20, 21, 115
Quincy Metal Fabricators, Inc., 5
Quincy Museum, The 5, 119
Quincy Park District, 113
Quincy Preservation Commission/ City of Quincy, 5
Quincy Preserves, 5
Quincy Public Library and Reading Room, 117
Quincy Society of Fine Arts, 5
Quincy Stove Manufacturing Company, 115
Quincy Whig, 120
Randolph, Smith M., 117
Reinecker House, Frederick and Leondine, 115
Reinecker, Frederick, 21, 22, 115
Reticker House, John and Mary, 124
Richardson House, William and Anna, 116
Richardson, H.H., 117
Richardson, W.A., 18
Ricker National Bank, 14, 116
Ricker, H.J.F., 23
Ridgewood Drive, 17
Rogers House, Edward and Elenora, 121
Ruff House, John and Casper, 115
Rupert, E.P., 124
Salem Evangelical Church, 14, 23, 116
Schemming's clothing store, 25
Schenk, Ferdinand, 120
Schenk, Henry, 115
Schmidt house, 121
Schurmeier Building, Johann, 115
Scott House, Samuel and Lida, 119
Seaside, Florida, 17
Silsbee, J. Lyman, 23, 117
Singleton, James W., 14
Skinner, Onias, 115
Snitjer House, Dricus and Fanny, 23, 116
South Park Pavilion, 124
South Park, 124
Southampton, New York, 17
Sprick House, Henry and Clara, 124
St. Boniface Church, 14
St. Francis Solanus Catholic Church, 116
St. John the Baptist Catholic Church, 14, 120
St. John's Episcopal Church, 22, 113
St. Pauli German Evangelical Lutheran Church, 116
St. Peter's Church, 14
St. Rose of Lima Catholic Church, 123
Stahl House, George and Mary, 120
State Savings Loan and Trust Company, 23, 120
State Theater, 25
Stevenson House, Walter and Dorothy, 124
Stevenson, John and Carolyn, 5
Stevenson, Walter, 25
Stewart, James B., 5, 17, 128
Still, Fr. Joseph A., 120

Stillwell Foundation, 5
Taft, Lorado, 124
Talmadge and Watson, 123
Taylor, Isaac, 117
Taylor, Mrs. Maurice M., 5
Temple B'nai Sholom, 14, 115
Terrel House, Benjamin and Electa, 113
Timothy Rogers Block, 117
Trapp Row, 119
Tubbesing, Frank, 22, 24, 120
Twain, Mark, 23
U.S. Courthouse and Post Office, 117
U.S. Land Office, 18
Union Block, 115
Unitarian Church, 24, 123
University of Illinois, 24
Upjohn, Richard, 22, 113
Villa Kathrine, 121
Wabash Coal Company, 123
Wabash Line, 19
Wabash Railway Depot, 19
Waide, Milton, Photographic Studio, 121
Wallace House, Joanna R., 116
War of 1812, 18
Warfield House, William and Malvina, 117
Warfield house, 116
Warfield, William S., 14, 23, 24
Washington Park Bandstand, 124
Washington Park, 21, 22, 23, 124
Washington School, 123
Washington Square, 115
Washington Theater and Offices, 25, 124
Weis, Mrs. Henry B., 5
Wellman and Dwire Tobacco Company, 15
Wells House, George and Sarah, 123
Wells, Edward and Mary, 113
Wewer, Fr. Adrian, 115, 116
WGEM/AM/FM/TV, 5
Williams, Barbara Lindsay, 5
Williams, Dennis R., 5
Williamson House, Charles and Emily, 117
Wilms House, Frederick and Anna, 123
Wolff, Br. Anselm, 115
Women's City Club, 113
Wood House, Ernest and Clara, 121
Wood Mansion, John and Ann, 20, 21, 113
Wood, Ernest M., 22, 24, 25, 120, 121, 123
Wood, Ernest, Office and Studio, 123
Wood, John, 14, 15, 17, 18, 20, 113
Woodruff, I. O., 14
World War I, 19
World War II, 20
WPA Guide to Illinois, 19
Wright, Frank Lloyd, 23, 24, 25, 117, 123, 124
YWCA, 113
Zimmerman, Sharon, 5
Zwick Row, 124

RICHARD PAYNE

Richard Payne, FAIA, architectural photographer and architect, first practiced architecture in his native state of Texas before switching to professional photography. His assignments for many of the nation's leading architects have taken him throughout the United States and to Mexico, Canada, Europe, and the Middle East. His photography has been featured in more than a dozen exhibitions, and highlight such publications as *The Woodlands, Philip Johnson/John Burgee Architecture: 1979-1985, Landmarks of Texas Architecture, Historic Galveston, Johnson/Burgee Architecture,* and *Photography for Architecture.* Mr. Payne is a Fellow of the American Institute of Architects.

PAUL CLIFFORD LARSON

Paul Clifford Larson, consultant and writer with specialities in historic building research and design, is a past executive director of Quincy's Gardner Museum of Architecture & Design. He has conducted extensive National Register and historic site-survey work, has curated a variety of exhibits, and has published numerous articles and brochures dealing with historic architecture. Mr. Larson lives in St. Paul, Minnesota.

JAMES B. STEWART

James B. Stewart, a native of Quincy, is a Harvard Law School graduate and a former front-page editor of *The Wall Street Journal.* He won a Pulitzer Prize in 1988 for his reporting of the 1987 stock market crash and insider trading scandals. His books include *Den of Thieves, The Partners, The Prosecutors,* and his current book, *Blood Sport.* Mr. Stewart lives in New York City.

CARL LANDRUM

Carl Landrum, Quincy historian, is a former high school band conductor and retail music store owner, whose interest in researching the history of music in Quincy lead to the publication of several books over the years, including *Quincy in the Civil War, Quincy: A Pictorial History,* and *Gem City, A Quincy Scrapbook.*

HERRING PRESS

Herring Press was established in 1984 as a publisher of high-quality visual books designed and produced by Jerry Herring and Herring Design, his Houston-based graphic design firm formed in 1973. Herring Design has won major design awards throughout the country and has been featured in publications in the U.S., Europe and Japan. Herring Press has published five large-scale photographic works: *Houston, A Self-Portrait, Historic Galveston, Santa Fe, Mariotti,* and *Presence, The Transco Tower,* three histories: *The University Club of Chicago, Memorial Park* and *Fulbright & Jaworski;* two design books: *100 Texas Posters* and *Design in Texas;* and two guidebooks: *Houston Architectural Guide,* co-published with the AIA, Houston Chapter, and *Jerry Herring's Guide to Houston.* Mr. Herring has also written, designed, and produced two books for New York publisher Watson-Guptill: *Creative Self Promotion* and *Annual Report Design.*